Saira Anwar is from Manchester, England and is trained and qualified as a nursery nurse, childminder/centre worker.

She is also a recognised creative poet and author. Dedicating her time to writing and sharing inspirational content online, through her service 'Saira Anwar Inspired Poetry'. She continues to inspire many people everyday.

She has had several poems recognised for creativity, originality, imagery and expression - as a result she has had many published works to date.

The Death of a Beautiful Dream

A POETRY COLLECTION

Saira Anwar

Copyright © 2014 Saira Anwar

All rights reserved. No part of this book may be reproduced in any form or by any electronic or mechanical means including photocopying, recording, and information storage and retrieval systems - expect in the case of brief quotations embodied in articles or reviews - without written permission from the author.

Published and written by:
Saira Anwar Inspired Poetry (www.sairaanwar.co.uk)

Book & Cover design by:
ImLegallyDesigned (imlegallydesigned@gmail.com)

ISBN-13: 978-1494280635

ISBN-10: 1494280639

Printed in the US/UK

Saira Anwar
Facebook: fb.com/inspiredpoetry
Twitter: @sairaanwar786
Instagram: poetess_786

DEDICATION

To all my sisters in humanity

To my beloved parents, brother and sisters

To all my family and friends who have supported me throughout my poetic journey, including:

Mubashir (without whom this project would not be a reality), Maleeha, Aneesa Tahir, Sania and Isma, Kaamilah, Afsha and Aisha Farook, Aneesa Hussain and Sonia Iqbal

And most of all the One who has guided me throughout my life. I dedicate all my endeavours to Allah, and that it be accepted.

CONTENTS

Introduction	8
The Untold Journey	11
The Ocean of Hopes and Dreams	12
The One with the Blue Thobe	14
Candlelit Under Moonlight	18
Withered Emotion	19
Hidden Mask	22
A Beautiful Lie	26
The Death of a Beautiful Dream	28
Breaking Free	30
Blossom For Change	31
All The Wiser	33
The Strong Roses Bloom Once Again	35
The Fragrant Red Rose	37
Women	40

A Gift from a Sister	43
The Wilted Rose	45
Mirror	46
Winter Woes	48
Pearl of The Ocean	50
Fate	53
Footprints	54
The Reality of Love	56
The Expression of Poetry	59
Mums Are Forever	61
Family Ties	63
True Friendship	64
Crowning Glory	66
A Candle Shining Bright	68
Inspiration	70

INTRODUCTION

For me poetry is a form of expressing feelings, pain, and experiences in life, whilst connecting with the readers. My poetic journey has been exactly that, yet whilst that is the case, it has been a great form of therapy. A source of light, hope, self-reflection and inspiration. It has also given me a boost of confidence. So poetry is really a lot more than just words.

My one and only desire is to be an inspiration to everyone and seek inspiration through others, in hope that people may learn from experiences in life. The vision of inspiration I have is to be a voice that echoes mainly towards sisters in humanity, to the many wonderful women out there. My primary aim is to be a voice of support to them in anyway possible.

There is a reason why I have this vision.

Before I began writing, I made a life changing mistake which involved me leaving my family behind in England, and moving to unfamiliar lands down under. I left depressed and traumatised whilst there. These experiences are sometimes reflected in my work. We have to remember that anything can happen in life but what matters is how we deal with it. We cannot always get what we want; sometimes what we 'think' is good for us, may in fact be the opposite. I want to try and prevent others making the same mistakes.

So this led me to write this collection of poetry that I have chosen to name "The Death of a Beautiful Dream." The poems featured in this book take you through the journey, and the poetry essentially draws upon the lessons to be taken from each experience.

The collection covers a variety of themes most predominantly those of love, marriage, betrayal, friendship and family ties. Focusing on the cruel realities of relationships, the poems express the hardship accompanying life changing experiences.

I hope that you enjoy the poems, share it with others and most of all, I hope the poems bring about a birth of a beautiful dream for you, not the death of one. The poetry is aimed to be inspirational and educational, so I hope it does inspire and educate you.

So it is time now, for you to begin to read through the words of this journey. As you read each poem, do not just read the words but listen to them. Let the words internalise your being and translate the words into action.

Saira Anwar
Inspired Poetry
2014

The Death of a Beautiful Dream

The Untold Journey

Like poet's hidden amongst the light of creativity,

Thoughts, images, expression all monument plot!

Feelings cannot be bought; life is ever so short!

The rays of the sun flare so brightly.

Moonlight so dim; O so misty!

This journey is sublime; a journey untold.

Life's adventure; mysteries unfold.

This exciting journey is the opening to new pastures.

Life's journey; our experiences untold.

For few this is untold, nay! We think never so blue!

Morning rays shining bright,

All tuneful, beatful, as music plays in rhythm.

Shades of our past buried deep in the ground,

Our future awaiting us is ever so bright!

The Ocean of Hopes and Dreams

I walk alone and find myself walking through the ocean waves,

where no one has ever been before.

Together the ocean waves whirl, and

smack over the golden sand.

The ocean of dreams, the ocean of hopes,

that's further placed upon thy heart.

Within the deepness of the ocean lies a silent breeze,

of hopes and dreams; where you can find

faith and peace, even when you do not dream.

As the existence of hopes and dreams lie within,

you take a leap and immerse yourself in its deepness.

The ocean of hopes and dreams begin to sink in.

Upon this vast ocean; me a lonely soul.

Over the ocean waves and across the beach sand,

I found myself where no one had ever been before.

The ocean of hopes and dreams,

where my untold journey began.

The One with the Blue Thobe

An innocent looking stranger

came to the door at noon, and

he spoke with ulterior motives:

a hidden agenda under his sleeves.

He bore a navy blue thobe, and

for all he was kind and caring at first.

He asked more with the lips than with the eyes, and

he turned and looked at all who

sat that mysterious, awkward noon,

suspicious without a glance.

The tulip came forth onto the veranda

with let us look at the beautiful stars in the moonlight.

Pondering what of the noon to be,

the innocent stranger and I the tulip.

The ocean was whispering waves,

crashing against the shores.

Winter, yes, the winter waves were smacking my face,

the innocent looking stranger I wish I had known.

The tulip stood in the moonlight alone,

bent over the winter waves,

her face metamorphosised into a fake smile, and

the frightened thought of the hearts whisper.

The Death of a Beautiful Dream

The conniving stranger

wormed his way like a snake, and

speaking words of kindness.

He pierced her heart with words of love,

and blinded her eyes with his devilish charms.

Like a hawk he eyed his prey, and

swept her away to his cage.

She looked at him with her innocent eyes,

trying to understand his sweet lies.

She lived a dream of fantasy,

building so many hopes and dreams

to spend her life in eternity

with the man of her dreams.

She never knew his personality,

until it was exposed in reality.

A mysterious man in the navy blue thobe,

left her feeling lost in the dark.

Candlelit Under Moonlight

The red rose petals lay scattered

across the long red carpet trail on the floor,

the numerous sparkling stars, and

the moon so round and visible.

The ocean waves whispering waves of love,

in tune from their romantic candle lit for two.

With many miles to cross till the sandy shores appear,

two beloved hearts begin beating in rhythm

to one another as they gaze

into each other's eyes, like exuberant stars.

It takes only a drop of the cool breeze ocean

to give them all the peace they desire.

Withered Emotion

The fragrant flower let out a beautiful smell

as it entered the door.

His bright smile

illuminated the room for all to see.

Through the daisy flower blossomed

what we call 'love'.

It blazed through her veins, and

touched her heart,

as the tall figure entered the door,

her heart crumbled and melted to the floor.

He's what they call an angel out of this realm.

He's what every girl dreams of now and again.

The Death of a Beautiful Dream

This man caught her eye, and

swept her off her feet,

taking her far away across the Earth.

Soon he became a 'mysterious man,'

who hid his agenda and planned,

so that no one may know his reality.

He was but a 'charmer,' a man of deceit.

As he entered the door,

the rose he held was alive like spring.

His love gave life to the dead plant

in the dark night.

It gave life to an empty desert

that was deprived of its water.

However his love was a lie, and

his lie was covered up with pretentious love.

As he left the room

the plant he carried

died too.

Hidden Mask

I am very content and happy

at the thought, of marrying a man;

I do not even know.

Failing to see through lies,

my eyes blinded,

I go along, and

marry a man I do not even know.

They walk in with pretend faces,

all happy and content, acting

in their places.

Kind at first, and

now they complain;

and complain, but never give.

Life taught me that, marriage;

is great and not so tough.

However my experience,

is a tragic mistake.

Yesterday I was heedless to advice,

today I am the victims of lies.

Look!

Be careful, and

do not make the same mistake.

Be grateful of the advice you've got.

We always forget that, but never take heed.

I scream aloud to warn you now!

Follow my advice as it is profound.

The Death of a Beautiful Dream

I've decided to leave this man behind.

He has left me with a thirst; longing

for a partner to quench this thirst.

This pain I carry

is nothing but grief.

Yet now they wish to listen, when at first

they did not want to know even a dot.

I cried and cried

until my eyes went blind, but

it's the silence that I carry

that they find.

For I speak

to them no more.

Only I experienced this,

no one could ever know;

This pain I tell this pain I told.

Yesterday I was heedless to advice.

Today I am the victims of lies.

So listen to my advice

or be a victim of lies.

A Beautiful Lie

They say love is a flower, but

I experienced a thorn.

They say love is a memory, but

I experienced a tragedy.

Yet we say love is a feeling

of never letting go, and

holding tight until,

we are compelled to let go.

The experiences we face

can be a mistake, but

it's we must learn from them.

You see life

is full of opportunities, but

we need to pick the right one

when it comes along.

Don't allow a negative experience to

pull you down.

Learn to let the hurt inside go, and

let your inside be sound.

Those who hurt us want to destroy us.

Let us pick ourselves up and

strive to achieve our full potential.

The Death of a Beautiful Dream

I once had a dream of the crème de le crème fairy tale world.

Sitting amongst the starlight waiting to be found.

Seated on the flower bed with different flowers;

White roses, red roses, tulips,

carnations and orchids,

I shined like a crown of jewels

where I glowed like a star on a hot summer's day

waiting to depart.

She's a beautiful rose,

He's a conniving chameleon.

When the traumatised heart collapsed at noon, and

with the white dove now a prisoner,

he labelled her like poison

with torture and pain,

he did not stop but label, and

terrorise her to come again at twilight.

He was a stormy wind,

tattered with an unevenness with which

he himself could not cope.

No rose could know, but

he cackled evilly upon the wounded.

He gave the sorrowed a mimic, and

a horrified glare, like the tyrants

who lay within that dark mysterious, and

spooky night asleep.

Deviously he half provoked her to stop

for the suffocation and escape.

Breaking Free

I was a seeker on my path to love, and
someone who was ripped apart, broken
by what I thought was love.
I shut myself from the world, and
thought I would never seek love again.
Heartbroken in despair, my pain
became my prison, and
one day it occurred to me;
that I ought to express myself
through letters and words.
Like this, I discovered my path
to letting it all out and letting go.

Blossom for Change

Peoples looks and lies can be so deceiving, and

ever so misleading.

Lies can be so blinding, leaving you

in a dark surrounding.

The deceit of peoples looks and lies,

are but an illusion, that send you

into state of delusion.

Yet liars themselves can be deluded,

trying to create the illusive.

Peoples looks and lies can be so deceiving;

What's wrong with their lives?

The liar came at me like an arrow,

The Death of a Beautiful Dream

casting his shadow, but Loo-Hoo-Ser!

You totally missed the plot!

I dodged, I coped, I hoped, and

my hope to cope changed me.

Even though my scars

remained with me,

the pain I gained, stayed

the same.

Through that very pain my life

blossomed, I changed.

I gained a life where

'I' became.

All The Wiser

Sometimes people say things, and

do things to hurt us, and try to poke fun.

Yet to them our hurt is

like a golden glow.

We listen and laugh, yet

they scratch our backs, and

treat us like crack.

Yet our hurt still in tact.

In the end we are victims, but

through it we grow all the wiser.

They on the other hand,

remain as they are;

only losing out like

a candle of melting wax.

If you're not going to become all the wiser,

then at least let someone know

of the pain you endure.

With some help,

you can become all the wiser, and

overcome the trauma;

you will come to realise then,

what a relief it is.

The Strong Roses Bloom Once Again

From a garden of roses emerged beautiful roses,

their beauty, stamina, courage, and strength

attracted the sweetest of petals.

Such sweetness and strength helped inspire.

Each petal represents our soft skin and essence.

The stems represent our strength and courage.

The leaves represent our sadness and burden.

The petals represent our stamina and beauty.

We, those roses, have not shown the best of us yet.

Life has worked us relentlessly

destroying every fibre of our being, but

we will fight it to our death.

The Death of a Beautiful Dream

The best of us is worth seeing.

We roses were once heartbroken,

we endured the pains of thorns,

hid amidst its terror, we fought

for life and picked ourselves up

time and time again, and

blossomed into the beautiful

strong roses we were once again.

The Fragrant Red Rose

So the rose we awaited,

finally came to surface.

When the fragrant red rose

suddenly appeared, her beauty

attracted the sweetest of thorns, and

her love imprisoned the hearts of many souls.

A rose craves its water, with

every rose scented petal

representing our soft skin.

The solid stem; our strength.

The fragrant red rose; so pure and sweet.

The leaves represent our burden,

sadness, courage, and essence.

The Death of a Beautiful Dream

Everytime you look at the fragrant red rose,

remember how beautiful and special we are.

A rose blooms for eternity within

our hearts and memories.

Everything seems endless for us.

All else appearing to wither expect us.

The rose fills our lives with a beautiful aroma.

It shines only when it's given a rosy smile.

Roses are a dream come true

only when you truly believe.

It's a seed that blooms,

only when it's planted' and

allowed to grow over time.

It's like friendship;

we don't realise its 'beauty' until it fades.

It's a lamp which leaves an eternal glow,

only when we know,

it will heal our hearts.

Rose is a lantern which heats,

only when we need the warmth of it.

Women

Women are precious like gems.

Like a rose with their beautiful petals,

glistening in the starlight, and

so transparent that you can see inside them.

Through their glistening gem-blazed petals,

women are like crown of jewels, where

they shine like a star during a full moon.

In the lost path,

women are like diamonds waiting to be found.

Women hide and carry so much burden,

fear, sadness, and tears, but

it reflects one thing; that's 'strength'.

We are like a surface of glass,

the more you wipe us gently, the more

we will shine like diamonds, and

we will see our reflections shining through,

as if we are preserving our images

inside of us ever so shyly.

If we are broken in one day,

it will be so hard to collect the shattered pieces again.

If you were able to collect the pieces, even then

we will not be the same as we once were.

We will always be disfigured.

The Death of a Beautiful Dream

Every time your hands pass

through our fracture zones;

'Scars'

It will leave a mark like tar.

The bruises will be hidden in the dark.

Like darkness covering the night,

the bruises are hidden deep inside.

A Gift from a Sister

You're beautiful like a fragrant red rose

Your eyes sparkle like the starlight

Your face glows like rose petals

You shine like a crown of jewels

You're a summer's rose

Your inner beauty continues to flow,

touching our souls.

You're the light of our eyes.

You fill our hearts with

so much love and compassion.

Having you as my sister

means so much more to me.

The Death of a Beautiful Dream

Our relation is like a rose,

may the beauty of it never fade,

like a rose which blooms for eternity.

Our relation is a close tie

that holds us together.

It's an album of reminiscences,

which you can look through.

You're precious like a gem.

The Wilted Rose

Through the wilted rose blazed radiant pain.

All lost in hope and despair.

She looked through her empty eyes.

She was like the meadows, where

a lonely woman seeks a companion.

Her beautiful eyes had lost their sparkle.

The loss she expressed was no longer there.

Through the rose blossomed a beautiful flower.

The rose that hid amidst the pain of thorns,

fought for her life and picked herself up again

and the wilted rose

blossomed into a beautiful

strong rose once more.

Mirror

We hide what we do not want to show.

Appearances can portray a sense of strength.

Yet behind that appearance,

we find something far from strong.

Crumbling on the inside and the outside,

trapped in our persona,

our every thought tainted

by memories of our look.

Nothing can take away the pain of

looking in the mirror crying, because

we hate what is staring back at us.

All we see are imperfections, and an empty heart.

We pretend to lead a perfect life, but

nothing is what it seems.

Our appearance is slipping,

to a state we can no longer bear.

Suffocated by our fears of what is in the mirror,

until we can hide it no more.

This unbearable fear we call; 'appearance'

with which we deal behind closed doors.

Winter Woes

It's winter woes, winter woes,

when everyone wraps up warm.

People under a warm fireplace.

People feeling on a low.

It's winter's woes, winter woes,

when it's freezing with a cold breeze.

When everyone's down

like a snowy day.

It's winter woes, winter woes.

It's freezing cold and so foggy.

Some people looking forward

to the snow.

It's winter woes, winter woes.

We all got the runny nose,

red and sore from blowing, hey ho!

The snow is coming,

Cars don't start in the morning,

frozen paths and roads,

its the winter's woes.

Pearl of the Ocean

Love is like a pearl of the deep ocean radiating the heart.

Love is like the ocean that whisper's words of love to two loving hearts.

Love is like a dove that whisper's words of love to two beloveds.

It's like the starlight that awaits a companion,

shining like a crown of jewels, and glowing like a star.

Love is like a tropical breeze in the hot heat on our journey to love.

It has an eternal glow.

It's like the bright sun that radiates our day.

Love is like a mine of jewels, that opens the deep ocean within our hearts.

Love will always find its way through all languages on it's own.

Love is growing as a couple, learning about each other, and not giving up on each other.

When we are truly in love being loving, caring, understanding, and pure, and most of all it's about being true.

It's about sacrificing ourselves.

Love is the light of our souls, the beat of our hearts.

Love is the light of our eyes.

We desire to seek and meet 'the one.'

Our hearts are filled with so much love and compassion.

Love is like the radiant star when compared to the moon.

The Death of a Beautiful Dream

It's like diamonds compared to the stones.

It's like rubies and pearls compared to the jewels.

Love is so beautiful and radiant that blazes passion, and

it grows and grows deeper.

Love is a special connection between people.

It's a special chemistry that comes out of the blue.

Love is a mystery that keeps us waiting.

Love is being with someone that isn't afraid to admit they miss us.

Someone that knows we are not perfect, but treats us as we are.

Someone who can't imagine losing us.

Someone who gives their heart to you completely.

Someone that says 'I love you' and proves it, and

someone who still falls in love with us all over again.

Love is not about finding someone who likes us.

It's about finding someone that completes us.

Fate

Fate is believing and seeking.

It's by chance and glance.

It's meant to be and will be.

Fate decides who we meet in our destiny.

Fate crops up when you least expect it.

Fate is in the hands of the Almighty.

Fate can mean a thousands things.

Fate can change at any time.

Fate will always decide whether

we live another day.

Fate grips you by the hand.

And decides your ultimate end.

Footprints

People come and go in your life.
Some of them are special to you, and
some of them you wish to forget.

They always give you emotional scars,
left to linger on in life, yet
the pain always remains the same.

But right now; you are a strong warrior.
Through the pain you experienced
you came to blossom.

You never lost hope;
Blossoming,

As you knew one fact;

That in tough times, there is always a chance,

that there is a lot you will gain.

And one day, see the change.

People come and go in your life, yet

it's the special memories,

that always leave the footprints behind.

And the special ones will

always leave an unforgettable mark on your heart.

Look out for them, and always wish to be one of them.

The Reality of Love

Love is like a rainbow it radiates my soul.

Love is the like the sun that sends out a glow.

Love is like the singing birds

that hymn in the sun.

Love is like a cool breeze in the scorching heat.

On my path to love, I experienced obstacles and barriers.

As I fell to the ground on my knees,

the obstacles prickled deep inside me.

However I picked myself up, and

continued on my journey to love.

I will continue to love,

for love sets me free.

Love is much too powerful

for us to hold or see.

It's sweet and pure, but

is love true?

Well that depends on the person, because

they will lie, and pretend

to love and comfort you.

This I do believe.

So we must look carefully before we fall deep.

That the person is pure, but most of all true.

As love can be pure and sweet, or, sour and kind.

But is it true?

The Death of a Beautiful Dream

This depends on the mood and nature;

we must remember that if he's true,

there wouldn't be any lies

and sour moods.

Just sweet moods, and

cherishable memories of a true love.

But what is true love? Well

that depends on you.

True love is a special connection between the two;

it is a special feeling that comes out of the blue.

True love is something that never can come true,

it's based on imagination and a dream come true.

Expression of Poetry

I have been writing for a very long time.

I have had a lot of time to express my inner deep feelings.

Poetry is a form of expression.

It's a work of expression, imagery, creativity and originality.

I'll write by an ocean view penthouse

under the candlelight on vanilla coloured sheets, and

there I will continue writing my poetry

in a spectacular style and inspire the globe.

Until daylight dawns upon this beauty of writing once again.

I shall awake and arise once more like a creative poet.

Poetry is a form of expression.

I have answered all their hurt hidden within my poems.

The Death of a Beautiful Dream

Now that I am ready to take on the world by storm, and

that finally, I'm a strong woman; know

that I will always be here

with my inspired poetry.

Mums Are Forever

Mums always remember so well

all the things they did together with their children.

All the subjects they discussed.

All the fun they had.

Mums always remember how

their love and friendship

is such a stabilising force

during all the hard times in their lives.

Mums may have different lifestyles.

Live in different places and interact with different people.

But, no matter how their lives may change.

Their love and friendship will always remain the same.

The Death of a Beautiful Dream

We know throughout our lives wherever we are.

We will always remember so well, and

cherish our mothers love and friendship

as one of the best we have ever known.

Family Ties

Families are a close tie that hold us together.

Our relation is like a rose,

may the beauty of it never fade, and

like a rose may it bloom for eternity.

Families are like diamonds compared to the stones.

Like the radiant star compared to the moon.

Families are the light of our eyes.

They fill our hearts with so much love and compassion.

True Friendship

Friendship is a rare jewel that shines, only when

We give it a sunny smile.

Friendship is a lock that opens, only when

We unlock our true selves to it.

Friendship is a path which we will find, only when

We know we are lost.

Friendship is a hand that holds us together, only when

We extend ours.

Friendship is an album of memories we can leaf through, only when

We cherish it.

Friendship is like a rose, only when

we realise it's beauty fading away.

Friendship is of many languages, only of which

We can speak.

Friendship is a potpourri of many feelings, only which

We can feel and smell.

When we have true friends, it's only when

We know the meaning of

'True Friendship.'

Crowning Glory

From the beautiful crystal palace emerged

a beautiful princess named 'Asiya.

She had beautiful, long golden luscious silky hair, and

very striking hazel green eyes.

She lived in a crystal palace with her parents, sisters and brothers.

Their beauty and persona attracted the sweetest of thorns.

She stood out on her balcony in her jade green glowy attire,

with her fancy jewelled crown at noon.

Princess 'Asiya was a beautiful girl; a ray of the sun,

the most elegant and beautiful of princesses; a glowy star, and

a diamond in a blue clear sky.

Each stone representing personality.

The diamonds representing beauty.

The rubies and emeralds representing their courage,

stamina, and strength.

Every time you look at the crown, remember how much we glow,

and how beautiful we are.

Princess 'Asiya lived a dream of hope and fantasy,

building so many dreams and desires

with her parents, sisters and brothers.

A handsome prince in the glowing attire

swept her off her feet and spent eternity

happily in paradise together.

A Candle Shining Bright

Sparkling and shimmering the candle glows,

my hopes and dreams twirling

in the vibrant starry skies.

Like a graceful poet, the light glows and sways,

my hope and thoughts mesmerised,

by the silent words.

Its beauty reflects through the words of my soul,

I feel positive energy and joy, I feel hopeful.

This tiny flame casts its light,

illuminating the world,

What an inspiration to embrace!

Let my heart be like the candle spreading

its light of joy, compassion, and inspiration.

Let it reflect in the hearts of many

to awaken our hearts, and live in the light

to be the light forever shining bright.

Inspiration

Today the beauty of early dawn came over me, and

I wondered who my words of wisdom would reach out to.

Then this morning I pondered once again.

Who am I?

What am I?

What is my purpose as I write?

A poet you may say, or a writer you may say.

Yes, I am someone who writes; getting poetic

With inspiring words of poetry

Much to your delight,

Words that move millions mightily

Because they're enlightened with hope.

We all seek inspiration from many sources, but

Are there any mightier than the word?

These are the words of wisdom

'I' voice.

This is

'Inspiration'.

Printed in Great Britain
by Amazon